TREES

EVERGREEN TREES

John F. Prevost
ABDO & Daughters

Published by Abdo & Daughters, 4940 Viking Drive, Suite 622, Edina, Minnesota 55435.

Copyright © 1996 by Abdo Consulting Group, Inc., Pentagon Tower, P.O. Box 36036, Minneapolis, Minnesota 55435 USA. International copyrights reserved in all countries. No part of this book may be reproduced in any form without written permission from the publisher.

Printed in the United States.

Cover Photo credits: Peter Arnold, Inc.
Interior Photo credits: Peter Arnold, Inc.

Edited by Bob Italia

Library of Congress Cataloging-in-Publication Data

Prevost, John F.
  Evergreen Trees / John F. Prevost.
    p. cm. -- (Trees)
  Includes index.
  Summary: Provides basic information about evergreens and cone-bearing plants, including their structure, economic uses, and the pests and diseases that affect them.
    ISBN 1-56239-616-1
  1. Conifers--Juvenile literature. 2. Evergreens--Juvenile literature [1. Conifers. 2. Evergreens.] I. Title. II. Series: Prevost, John F. Trees.
  QK494.P74 1996   96-6062
  585'.2--dc20   CIP
                                                                       AC

ABOUT THE AUTHOR
John Prevost is a marine biologist and diver who has been active in conservation and education issues for the past 18 years. Currently he is living inland and remains actively involved in freshwater and marine husbandry, conservation and education projects.

Contents

Evergreen Trees and Family

Evergreens are a special plant group. Throughout the year, they keep their green leaves.

The name evergreen refers to two plant groups. One group—the **pines**, **spruce**, **firs**, and **yews**—have **cones** instead of flowers. They are also called **conifers**. The other group, including **junipers**, have berries.

Most evergreens are trees. They include the largest living plant, the coastal redwood, which may grow over 400 feet (122 meters) high. Others are low growing shrubs that fit into **residential** yards.

Not all evergreens keep their leaves. The **larches** (tamaracks) and bald **cypress** lose their leaves in the fall.

A sitka spruce.

Roots, Soil, and Water

Evergreens pull water from the ground with their roots. Water contains **minerals** and other **nutrients** which the tree uses for food. Without enough food, the tree will not grow or make seeds.

The roots also keep the evergreen from falling over. Evergreens do best in **fertile** soil. They need **moderate** amounts of water.

Opposite page:
Evergreens need minerals
and nutrients to stay healthy.

Stems, Leaves, and Sunlight

The evergreen trunk supports the branches, stems, and leaves. Evergreens use sunlight to change water, **nutrients**, and air into food and **oxygen**. This process is called **photosynthesis**.

The trunk, branches, and stems connect the roots to the leaves. This allows water and nutrients to reach the leaves. Food produced by the leaves can then travel back to the roots.

The leaves of evergreen trees are needle or scale shaped. These needles continue photosynthesis, even in the winter. Most evergreens keep their leaves throughout the year. They replace a few leaves at a time all year long.

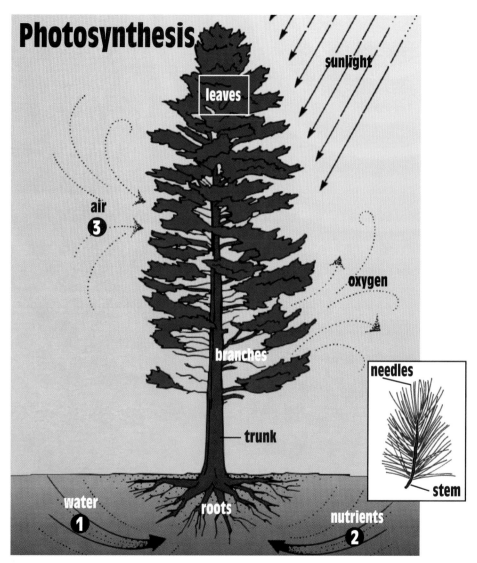

Ground water (1) and nutrients (2) travel through the roots, trunk, and branches and into the leaves (needles) where air (3) is drawn in. Then the tree uses sunlight to change these three elements into food and oxygen.

9

Flowers and Seeds

Evergreen "flowers" are called **cones**. The male cones are found high in the tree. They grow early in the spring when **pollen** is released.

The larger, female cones are often found on the ground under **pine** and **spruce** trees. These cones contain seeds. Some pine trees do not release the seeds until there is a fire. These seeds will **germinate** after forest fires, and will start a new forest.

Each seed contains a plant **embryo** and food. Under the right conditions, the seed will grow into another evergreen tree.

FEMALE CONE

scale

SCALE

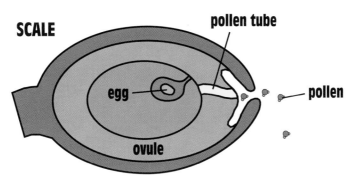

pollen tube

egg

pollen

ovule

Pollen from the male cone floats through the air to a scale of the female cone. Then the pollen enters the ovule through the pollen tube. There, the pollen fertilizes the egg, which grows into a seed.

Insects and Other Friends

Evergreen trees are home to hundreds of insects, spiders, and **mites**. Most help **pollinate** the tree or eat insect **pests.**

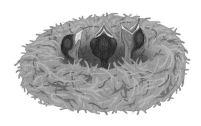

Birds make nests in evergreen trees.

Evergreens are also home to many birds and small **mammals** such as squirrels and chipmunks. Many nest within the leaves and branches and feed their young on pests.

In the winter, animals use the trees for shelter from the cold winds, and feed on hidden insect eggs.

Evergreens provide shelter and food for mammals and insects. Notice the fruits on this red cedar.

Pests and Diseases

Several insect **pests**, such as **aphids**, **mites**, and caterpillars, live on evergreen trees. Most do not threaten a healthy tree. **Predatory** insects such as wasps and ladybugs control these pests.

Diseases also attack weak evergreens that grow in bad soil. A healthy tree will resist diseases.

A ladybug feeds on pests.

Opposite page: Diseases attack weak evergreens and kill them.

14

Varieties

Most North American evergreen trees are members of the **pine family**. These are the pines, **spruces**, **hemlocks**, and **firs**. Pine tree **varieties** are grown for size, leaf color, and tree shape.

Pines have leaves shaped like needles. Spruces have short, needle-shaped leaves. Hemlocks have flat needles, small cones, and reddish bark. Firs have flattened branches with flattened, dark green leaves.

Opposite page:
Most evergreen varieties are members of the pine family.

Uses

Evergreens have many uses. **Pines** and other **conifers** are cut down for lumber used to build homes and make paper.

Thousands are grown, cut, and sold in Europe and North America as Christmas trees. We even eat pine nuts. Evergreens are also popular for **landscape** use.

Opposite page:
Evergreens are used to
build homes, for Christmas
trees, and landscaping.

Evergreen Trees and the Plant Kingdom

The plant kingdom is divided into several groups, including flowering plants, fungi, plants with bare seeds, and ferns.

 Flowering plants grow flowers to make seeds. These seeds often grow inside protective ovaries or fruit.

 Fungi are plants without leaves, flowers, or green coloring, and cannot make their own food. They include mushrooms, molds, and yeast.

 Plants with bare seeds (such as evergreens) do not grow flowers. Their seeds grow unprotected, often on the scale of a cone.

 Ferns are plants with roots, stems, and leaves. They do not grow flowers or seeds.

There are two groups of plants with bare seeds: conifers and ginkgos. Conifers grow cones that make seeds. Ginkgos grow fruit that have seeds.

Evergreens are found in several conifer families, including the pine family, redwood family, cedar family, and yew family.

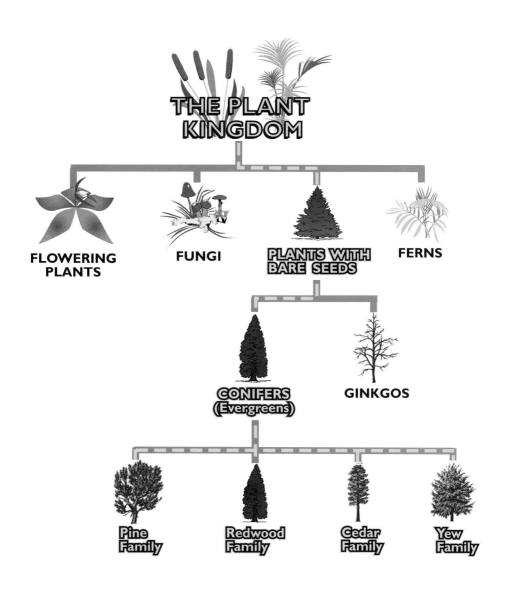

THE PLANT KINGDOM

FLOWERING PLANTS

FUNGI

PLANTS WITH BARE SEEDS

FERNS

CONIFERS (Evergreens)

GINKGOS

Pine Family

Redwood Family

Cedar Family

Yew Family

Glossary

aphid (AY-fid) - A small insect that sucks the sap from plant leaves and stems.

cone - The part that bears the seeds on a pine, cedar, and other evergreen trees.

coniferous (kuh-NIF-er-us) - Referring to cone-bearing plants.

cypress - An evergreen tree with small, dark-green leaves like scales.

disease (diz-EEZ) - A sickness.

embryo (EM-bree-oh) - An early stage of plant growth, before sprouting from a seed.

family - A group of related living things.

fertilize (FUR-tuh-lies) - To develop the ovule into a seed.

fir - An evergreen tree somewhat like a spruce, often used for Christmas trees.

germinate (JER-mih-nate) - A seed that is starting to grow.

hemlock - An evergreen tree with flat needles, small cones, and reddish bark.

juniper (JEW-nih-pur) - An evergreen shrub or tree with tiny bluish cones that look like berries.

landscape - To make land more pleasant to look at by arranging trees, shrubs, or flowers.

larch - A tree with small cones and needles that fall off in autumn.

mammal - A warm-blooded animal with a backbone that feeds its offspring milk.

mineral - Any substance that is not a plant, animal, or another living thing.

mite - A tiny animal related to the spider and has eight legs.

moderate (MAH-der-it) - Not too hot and not too cold.

nutrient (NOO-tree-ent) - Substance that promotes growth or good health.

oxygen (OX-ih-jen) - A gas without color, taste, or odor found in air and water.

pest - A harmful or destructive insect.

photosynthesis (foe-toe-SIN-thuh-sis) - Producing food using sunlight as the source of energy.

pine - A tree that bears cones and has evergreen leaves shaped like needles.

pollen (PAH-lin) - A yellow powder that fertilizes flowers.

pollinate (PAH-lih-nate) - To move pollen from flower to flower, allowing them to develop seeds.

predator (PRED-uh-tore) - An animal that eats other animals.

residential (rez-ih-DEN-shull) - Having something to do with homes.

spruce (SPROOS) - A kind of evergreen tree with leaves shaped like needles.

varieties (vuh-RYE-uh-tees) - Different types of plants that are closely related.

yew - An evergreen tree from Europe and Asia.

Index